POLAR CREATURES

Douglas County Library
720 Fillmore St.
Alexandria, MN 56308

POLAR CREATURES

Benita Sen

PowerKiDS press.

New York

Published in 2008 by The Rosen Publishing Group, Inc.
29 East 21st Street, New York, NY 10010

Copyright © 2008 Really Useful Map Company (HK) Ltd.

All rights reserved. No part of this book may be reproduced in any form without permission in writing from the publisher, except by a reviewer.
First Published: 2006
Designed by Q2A Media

Picture credits:
t: Top, m: Middle, b: Bottom

6, 8, 17: Silense, 7: Vera Bogaerts, 9t: Styve, 9b: spxChrome, 10b: Cindy Haggerty, 11b: Janugio, 14t, 14b, 18t,: National Oceanic & Atmospheric Administration (NOAA),U.S. Department of Commerce, 16b: Freezingpictures | Dreamstime.com, 20t, 20b, 21: U.S. Fish and Wildlife Service, 22br: Koval, 23t: zastavkin, 23b: Keith Levit, 24t: Loo Joo Pheng, 25b: Fernando Rodrigues, 29bl: Stephen Coburn, 34b, 35b: Ilya D. Gridnev: 34-35b: akautz, 36-37t, 37b, 38t: SF Photography, 36-37b: J. Norman Reid, 38b: Sword Serenity, 40b: Anyka, 40-41m: Halldor Eiriksson, 41t: Bryan Eastham, 43t: Peter Ivanov Ishmiriev, 43b: Keith Levit.

Library of Congress Cataloging-in-Publication Data

Sen, Benita.
  Polar creatures / Benita Sen.
    p. cm. — (Wild creatures)
  Includes index.
  ISBN-13: 978-1-4042-3892-3 (library binding)
  ISBN-10: 1-4042-3892-1 (library binding)
  1. Animals—Polar regions—Juvenile literature. I. Title.
  QL104.S46 2008
  591.75'86—dc22
                                         2007008669

Manufactured in China

CONTENTS

Life at the Poles	6
Polar Bear	8
A Bear's Life	10
Arctic Seals	12
Seals of Antarctica	14
Leopard Seal	16
Walrus	18
Caribou	20
More Arctic Animals	22
Antarctic Marine Life	24
Arctic Whales	26
Killer Whale	28
Greenland Shark	30
Penguins	32
Emperor Penguins	34
Other Antarctic Birds	36
Snowy Owl and Falcon	38
Feathered Visitor	40
Endangering Polar Life	42
Glossary	44
Further Reading	46
Index	47

LIFE AT THE POLES

The Arctic Circle marks the start of the most northerly part of the earth. The Antarctic Circle marks the start of the most southerly. North of the Arctic Circle and south of the Antarctic Circle are the polar regions. The South Pole is the coldest place on earth. The coldest temperature recorded was -129° F (-89.4° C).

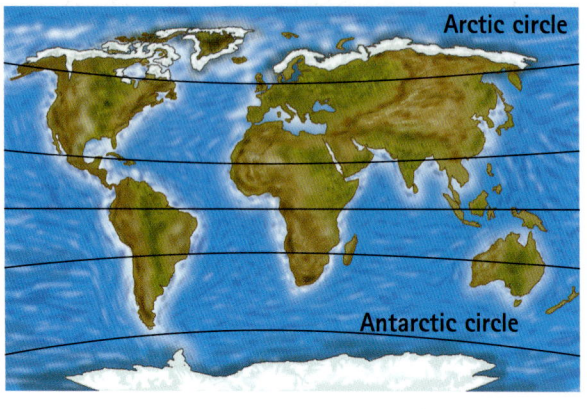

The areas marked in white show the Arctic and the Antarctic circles of the globe.

Poles apart

The Polar regions are also the most windy places on earth. Most of the land is covered with ice and snow. Summer comes to the North Pole around June and to the South Pole around December. During summer the polar regions have light 24 hours and no darkness. This is because the sun never sets. In winter however, the sun never rises, and there are days when it is dark for 24 hours.

The North Pole

Parts of the Arctic Ocean are frozen throughout the year and the average winter temperature is -22° F (-30° C). Even when the snow melts, the Arctic region is covered with permafrost, a frozen layer of soil just under the surface. Summers are warm enough for some plants to grow. The edge of the Arctic region, covered with short grass, is the tundra. In Finnish, *tunturia*, from which it gets its name, means "treeless plain."

The first expedition to the North Pole was made on April 6, 1909, by Robert Edwin Peary, Matthew Henson and four Inuit men.

The South Pole

Antarctica is larger than the United States. It is a frozen, dry and windy continent of glaciers and high mountains. The land is covered with ice about 1.2 miles (2 km) thick. The only people living there are scientists. The vegetation includes 400 types of lichen, 100 species of moss, 30 species of liverwort and around 700 types of algae. The only flowers that grow are hair grass and pearlwort. A few animals such as penguins, whales and seals live here. Squid and ice fish live in the sea. They are food for the albatross, one of the few birds that fly over Antarctica.

Cherish and conserve

Both the North Pole and the South Pole are being affected by pollution. The Great Arctic Reserve, set up by the government of Russia, is one of the largest protected areas in the world. Covering 17,760 square miles (46,000 sq km), it is a safe home for 700,000 reindeer, polar bears and seals. On the opposite Pole, the Southern Ocean that surrounds Antarctica has been declared an international whale sanctuary.

The first humans to reach the South Pole were Roald Amunsden and his party on December 14, 1911.

FACT FILE

North Pole

Full name	Arctic
Nearest landmass	Greenland, 450 miles (724 km) south
Water depth	13,500 feet (4,114 m)
Average temp.	-0.4° F (-18° C)
Ice thickness	3-6 feet (0.9-2 m)
Earliest explorers	Peary and Henson (1909)

South Pole

Full name	Antarctica
Area	5,501,925 square miles (14,250,000 sq km)
Coldest	-129° F (-89.4° C) at Vostok on July 21, 1983
Warmest	-31° F (-35° C)
Wind speed	Up to 199 miles per hour (320 km/h)
Earliest explorer	Roald Amundsen (1911)

POLAR BEAR

The polar bear is the largest meat-eating animal on land. It is the only animal that actively hunts humans. It is also the top predator in the Arctic region. It feeds on seals and walruses found in the region. Polar bears are found throughout the Arctic. They usually live on sea ice and along the shores.

Polar bears are so well protected that they often overheat. They move slowly to avoid overheating. Occasionally they swim to cool down.

Life in the North Pole

The polar bear is large and heavy. It has a small head, long neck, rounded ears and a short tail. The front legs of the polar bear are shorter than the hind legs. The large paws of the bear help spread its weight over a large area. This prevents the ice from breaking under the bear's weight. The bottom of the paws have thick, black pads covered with small bumps, called papillae. The fur and the papillae stop the bear from slipping on ice. Sharp, curved claws are used for extra grip while running or climbing as well as for grasping prey.

Keeping warm

The polar bear is well-adapted for its life in the cold Arctic region. It has a layer of blubber, about 4 inches (10 cm) thick. Blubber is a thick layer of fat found under the skin. It keeps the bear warm both on land and in water. The bear digs a hole in the snow and curls up in it during extremely cold and windy days. It also covers its nose and mouth with its paws on such occasions, so that heat does not escape through these areas. The bear's small ears and short tail also prevents heat loss. Apart from this, the bear has a coat that is about 2 inches (5 cm) thick.

Furry tales

From a distance, the polar bear looks white, even yellowish in color. The hair that covers the body of the polar bear is, in fact, colorless! The thick coat of the polar bear consists of a dense layer of underhair covered by a thinner layer of clear, hollow guard hair. The inner layer keeps the bear warm, while the guard hair directs sunlight into the inner layer. The outer guard hairs reflect light making the bear appear white.

A polar bear's hair can easily shake off water or ice after a swim.

A watery life

Polar bears are very good swimmers. They have been known to swim continuously for more than 60 miles (100 km) at speeds of about 6 miles per hour (10 km/h). Polar bears use their front paws as paddles while swimming. The paws are partially webbed for the same reason. The back legs of a polar bear are held flat and used to steer the bear. The layer of blubber keeps the bear warm while swimming. Polar bears are also known to dive, although they do not dive very deep.

CREATURE PROFILE

Common name:	Polar Bear
Scientific name:	*Ursus maritimus*
Found in:	The Arctic region (Alaska, Canada, Russia, Greenland, Norway)
Length:	Adult males – 8-10 feet (2.5-3 m)
	Adult females – 6.5-8 feet (2-2.5 m)
Prey:	Seals (ringed and bearded seals), bird eggs, sea birds, young walruses, dead whales and berries
Enemies:	Humans. Polar bears were hunted extensively for their thick fur and meat. Their long canine teeth were used to make jewelry and artifacts.
Status:	Threatened. Following strict laws, the polar bear population has now become stable. Today, there are about 40,000 polar bears in the Arctic.

A polar bear's nostrils close when it is under water

A BEAR'S LIFE

Polar bears have paw pads with rough surfaces. These help to prevent them from slipping on the ice.

Going for the kill

The polar bear is one of the best hunters in the bear family. Their favorite prey is ringed seals. They also kill the larger and heavier walrus and beluga whale. They often stand silently by a seal's breathing hole, waiting for it to surface. When the seal comes up for air, the polar bear flips it out with a blow of its large front paw. They sometimes stalk prey or swim beneath the ice looking for food.

What a good nose!

Polar bears have a good sense of smell that helps them in hunting. They can detect seal breathing holes covered by layers of ice and snow as far as 0.62 miles (1 km) away. They can see and hear about as well as a human and can swim underwater with their eyes open. An angry polar bear will hiss, snort, growl and roar. Cubs that act up are met with a low growl or a soft bat from their mother's paw.

Polar bears dig a hole in snow and cuddle up to keep themselves warm.

Polar bears have 42 teeth, which they use for catching food or for aggressive behavior and occasionally for displaying affection.

Happy birthday, baby bear!

Polar bears are born between the end of November and early January. Most mothers have two cubs at a time, but some have one or three. The cubs, born blind, weigh only 1.32 pounds (0.6 kg) and are covered with fine hair. They stay inside the den until early April, but do not leave their mother until they are two-and-a-half years old. She protects them during this time and teaches them to hunt. They grow very quickly between their first and second birthdays. They feed on their mother's milk, which has more fat in it than the milk of other bears. This helps them fight the cold.

Home, sweet home!

Mother bears prepare a den for their babies at one end of a tunnel. The opening to the tunnel is sealed with soft snow, which traps in air and keeps the den much warmer than outside. Once the cubs are a few months old, the family begins its journey back to the sea so that the mother can hunt for food. On the way, she digs resting pits in the snow to shelter her cubs from the freezing wind where they feed and rest.

Polar bears are extremely protective of their young ones. They risk their own lives in defending their cubs.

ARCTIC SEALS

Seals are sea mammals. Most seals live in or around the Arctic Circle or Antarctica. Seals are pinnipeds, or creatures that have flippers instead of limbs. Fur seals are the only seals that have an external ear. Seals are good swimmers, steering with their clawed front flippers and propelling themselves with their rear flippers. They are clumsy on land. Seals live in the coldest places in the world. A layer of blubber keeps them warm. There are six species of Arctic seals.

HARP SEAL

Harp seals are born with a yellowish fur. It remains yellow for three days, after which it turns white. This is why they are also called whitecoats. The white color helps them blend with the snow, but the silky, luxurious texture attracts enemies like humans. As the babies grow older, gray patches appear on the white fur. Harp seals get their name from the black horseshoe-shaped patch, or harp, on the back of adult males. Adult females have a lighter band. Harp seals can dive to 600-900 feet (182-275 m) and stay underwater for 15 minutes. Harp seals have a thinner neck than other seals. They swim in large herds of up to 75, diving and leaping.

My! You've grown!

They have a strong sense of smell, and the mother can sniff out her own pup from among many others. She nurses it for just two weeks. Her milk, rich in fat, helps the pup grow to about 88 pounds (40 kg) with a thick layer of blubber. This is about the time that pups are ready for their first swim. Harp seal pups are among the fastest growing mammals.

The black horseshoe-shaped patch on the Harp seal gives it the name.

HOODED SEAL

Hooded seals get their name from a black inflatable nasal sac on the male. They can inflate the hood and move air from one lobe to the other. Male hooded seals can also blow through one nostril to inflate a large red balloonlike skin, usually on the left nostril. They probably inflate the hood and blow the red balloon to impress female seals and to scare enemies away. They live alone, except when they molt, or shed their skin, from June to August.

Bye, mom

In March or April, females give birth to one pup that they nurse for only four to eight days, the shortest time for any mammal. These aggressive seals have gray blotches on their silvery-gray skin. The blue-gray pups have a thick layer of blubber and are called bluebacks. They shed this coat 14 months later.

Hooded seals are hunted for their oil, meat and skin, especially the thick pelts of newborn seals.

This harp seal and its pup are grovelling in the snow.

CREATURE PROFILE

Arctic seal

Length:	4 feet (1.25 m) in ringed seal - 10 feet (3 m) in adult male hooded seal
Weight:	110 pounds (49 kg) in ringed seal 880 pounds (400 kg) in adult male hooded seal
Prey:	Krill, squid, fish, octopus, mussels
Threats:	Humans, polar bear, orca, Greenland shark, wolverine, large birds, arctic fox, wolf, dog

SEALS OF ANTARCTICA

There are more seals in the Antarctic than in the Arctic. This is because the Antarctic has more food and fewer enemies for the seal. Seals live throughout the Antarctic region. The southern elephant seal is the largest. The adult males are 14–16 feet (4.5 m) long.

The Weddell, ross, crabeater and leopard seals are the only true seals, since they have no external ears.

WEDDELL SEAL

Named after the British Antarctic explorer James Weddell, these seals live in large groups on the ice. They spend most of their time underwater and come up to breathe and to give birth to their pups. Their dark silver-spotted coats have short, dense fur. They use their large canine teeth to scrape holes in the ice and to chew. Their whiskers help them swim around obstacles.

Deep divers

Weddell seals can dive over 2,000 feet (609 m) deep. They can stay under the water for an hour and call out loudly to each other under the water. Mother Weddell seals give birth to one pup around September. The pups grow from 60 pounds (27 kg) at birth to 200 pounds (90 kg) in eight weeks. By then, they have learned to swim, hunt and pull themselves out of water onto land. If they see another animal, they roll onto their backs in surrender.

CRABEATER SEAL

Crabeater seals have unusual five-point teeth that lock like a strainer to keep the aquatic food in when the water drains out. They eat krill, fish and squid, but not crabs. Their name is the result of a mistake an early scientist made. If another animal comes near, they bare their teeth and snort. Crabeaters can travel for about 35 miles (56 km) on land.

A change of wardrobe

Crabeater seals change their coats with the seasons. A dark gray in winter helps them retain heat. In summer, they turn white. The coat of crabeater seals is prominently scarred. These are scars of the wounds they receive from killer whales and leopard seals. They eat about twice their own weight of krill every month and can eat more krill than any of the baleen, or toothless, whales. They breed in small groups on the pack ice. Their pups have to grow fast so that they can look after themselves in barely three weeks. Crabeater seals are the most numerous seal species on the Southern Ocean.

CREATURE PROFILE

Antarctic seal

Length: Crabeater Seal 9–10 feet (2.7–3 m), Weddell seal 10.5 feet (3.2 m)

Weight: Crabeater seal about 500 pounds (226 kg), Weddell seal about 1,000 pounds (453 kg)

Prey: Krill, squid, fish

Threats: Leopard seal, orca

Crabeater seals molt in January and February. They spend most of their time on the ice when molting.

LEOPARD SEAL

The second largest of the Antarctic seals is the leopard seal. It has a long, slim, torpedo-shaped body. Its name comes from its gray fur spotted with black. It is the only seal that eats other seals. The female leopard seal, usually 9.84 feet (3 m) long, is larger than the male!

A good hunter

This seal has strong jaws, long, sharp teeth and a huge mouth. It also has sharp eyesight and can smell underwater. It is a powerful swimmer and makes a dangerous enemy for penguins and other seals swimming or resting on the ice. Its head looks more like a reptile's, with nostrils on top of its snout. Its neck and back are strong. Powerful front flippers help steer through the water at speeds of up to 25 miles per hour (40 km/h). They cannot move as easily on land. Their only enemy is the killer whale.

A varied menu

Their main food is penguins, but they also eat other seals, fish, squid, krill, sea birds and even platypus. They chew with long, pointed, inward-curving teeth. These sawlike teeth come in handy to tear off flesh or to sift out water when they catch krill. They swim fast and far, traveling more than any other seal, sometimes as far as South Africa and Australia.

Since leopard seals do not hunt in open water they do not need to dive for more than fifteen minutes.

On the surface, leopard seals appear more squat, while in the ocean they look longer and sleeker, like a snake.

Lone mother

Leopard seals live until they are about 26 years old. They live alone, except during the breeding season. A mother has one pup each season, which is born in a hole that she digs in the ice. The pups are born between November and January. The mother eats a lot before she leaves the water to give birth, so she can go for several days without eating. The pup is fed on fatty milk, and doubles in size in three months. Three weeks after birth, it is ready for its first swim and goes fishing for krill.

First human prey

Leopard seals rarely attack humans and even swim alongside scientists. But on July 22, 2003, a leopard seal attacked and killed British marine biologist Kirsty Brown, the first recorded human death. With more and more scientists going down to Antarctica, such attacks may increase. There are few threats to these animals, which number about 222,000. Its only enemy is the killer whale. A major threat for the leopard seal would be a drop in the amount of krill, which could happen if the seas of the Antarctic get more polluted.

CREATURE PROFILE

Common name:	Leopard seal
Scientific name:	*Lydrurga leptonyx*
Found in:	The Antarctic region, rarely straying up to South Africa, Australia
Weight:	Adult males: 705 pounds (320 kg)
	Adult females: 815 pounds (370 kg)
Length:	Adult males: 9.1 feet (2.8 m)
	Adult females: 9.8 feet (3 m)
Prey:	Penguins, other seals, fish, squid, krill, sea birds, platypus
Enemies:	Killer whales, humans

WALRUS

The walrus is an Arctic mammal, which has been around for at least 14 million years. It is very large. In fact, it gets its name from the Dutch words, *wal* (shore) and *reus* (giant). They can grow up to 14 feet (4 m) long, and have long tusks.

Heavier than a polar bear

A male walrus can weigh 1,764-3,748 pounds (800-1,700 kg) but it is the size of the ivory tusks that decides who is the dominant male. Both males and females have tusks. These help them to anchor on the bottom of the ocean (about 304 feet (95 m) deep) to dig for clams, snails, shrimps, worms and mussels. A walrus squirts jets of water to bring the clams out and can eat 4,000 clams in one meal. They feed twice a day, eating a quarter of their body weight each time. The tusks, which help them to crack breathing holes in the ice, have age rings. They are used to fend off polar bears and killer whales.

The longer the tusk of the walrus, the higher is its rank in the group.

Wowzee whiskers

A walrus can walk on its four fins.

The walrus has a bristly moustache with about 700 hairs in 13 to 15 rows that help it to feel its way underwater. Its thick, armorlike wrinkly skin changes from cinnamon brown or pink to almost white when the walrus is under the chilly water. A 3.9 inches (10 cm) layer of blubber or fat keeps them warm. They shed their short hair between June and August. Walruses have 18 teeth, including their tusks, two small eyes and small openings for ears. They have great hearing. Walruses breathe through their mouth and nostrils, which are just above their whiskers. A walrus swims about 4.3 miles per hour (7 km/h), but manages short bursts of up to 21.7 miles per hour (35 km/h).

Family animal

Walruses spend about two-thirds of their time in water and the rest on ice floes and beaches. Walruses seldom go out alone, though males and females gather in separate herds. A school of walruses can have more than 100 members that communicate with clacks, whistles, roars, growls, grunts, barks, rasps, knocks and even a bell-like underwater sound. A mother has one calf every two years, born on the ice, weighing about 99-165 pounds (45-75 kg) and about 3-4 feet (95-123 cm) long. The calf often takes a ride on the mother's back and gets milk upside down when the mother is in the water.

The walrus has a thick, wrinkly skin that acts like an armor, lending protection when it fights with other walruses.

Moving around

Walruses are pinnipeds, which means they have hairless flippers in place of limbs, like seals and sea lions. Their squarish front flippers have five fingers and help them steer in water. Their triangular back flippers also have five digits and act like a propeller. All four are used to walk on land. When they are tired of diving, walruses can fill up air sacs under their throat and float standing up!

CREATURE PROFILE

Common name:	Walrus
Scientific name:	*Odobenus rosmarus*
Found in:	Arctic region, 5-41° F (-15-5° C)
Weight:	Adult males: 1,764-3,748 pounds (800-1,700 kg)
	Adult females: 882-2,756 pounds (400-1,250 kg)
Length:	Adult males: 9-12 feet (2.7-3.6 m) long
	Adult females: 7.5-10 feet (2.3-3.1 m) long
Longevity:	35-50 years
Prey:	Clams, snails, shrimps, worms, mussels and rarely, young seals
Enemies:	Humans, polar bears, orca whales. Walruses were hunted extensively for fat and meat. Their tusks were used to make jewelry and artifacts.
Status:	Threatened. Laws ensure only people native to the Arctic may hunt them. About 250,000 walruses are left protected by laws in Russia and the United States.

CARIBOU

Caribou are ruminants. They are strong swimmers and can even sleep in the water. In winter, when food is snowed under, caribou shovel with their noses. Caribou are always on the move, looking for food.

Antlers for all

Caribou are the only member of the deer family in which both the male and female animals have antlers. The antlers begin to grow when a calf is just two months old. The antlers of male caribou are larger than those of the female. Their huge antlers spread about 4 feet (120 cm) across, are 4 feet 1 inch (125 cm) long and weigh 15-20 pounds (6.8-9 kg). They shed their antlers every year. From April to October, the antlers grow again from two stubs of bone, or pedicles. The new antlers are covered with soft fur called velvet. The velvet is cast off when the antlers have grown.

Special hooves

Caribou have large, wide hooves that support them in the snow and in the marshy tundra. The wide hooves distribute the caribou's weight as they walk over soft snow. In summer, when the tundra is wet and soft, the hoof pads are spongy. In winter, they tighten to keep the animal from slipping. Their hooves also help them paddle when they swim. Their legs are long, slim and strong. A calf begins to run 90 minutes after its birth to keep up with the herd. Veins and arteries run close together in the caribou's long legs. This helps to keep the blood of the veins warm as well. Their legs stay at a safe 86-122° F (30-50° C), which helps them survive the cold.

Caribou can travel up to 3,000 miles (4,828 km)!

CREATURE PROFILE

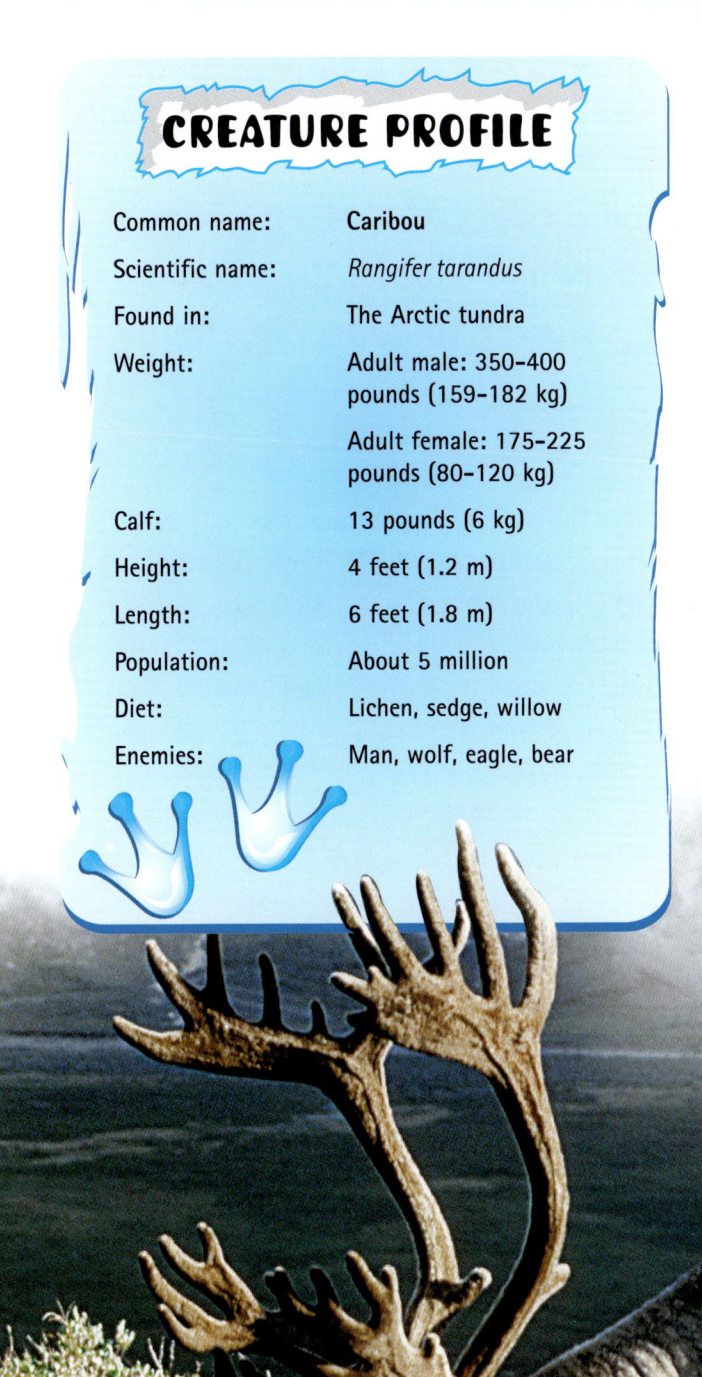

Common name:	Caribou
Scientific name:	*Rangifer tarandus*
Found in:	The Arctic tundra
Weight:	Adult male: 350-400 pounds (159-182 kg)
	Adult female: 175-225 pounds (80-120 kg)
Calf:	13 pounds (6 kg)
Height:	4 feet (1.2 m)
Length:	6 feet (1.8 m)
Population:	About 5 million
Diet:	Lichen, sedge, willow
Enemies:	Man, wolf, eagle, bear

A hearty meal

Caribou move in large herds. They eat up most of the food in one place and have to move on to find more food. In summer (May-September), caribou eat the leaves of the tiny willow, sedge, a grasslike plant, and flowering tundra plants. In winter, which sets in around October, most plants wither away. Caribou will then eat lichen, dried sedge, mushrooms and small shrubs.

What a long nose!

The caribou's nose is so long that by the time the cold air from outside travels to the animal's lungs, it becomes warm. The nose also gives the caribou a strong sense of smell to make up for its poor eyesight. Although they cannot tell apart an enemy from a friend until they are very close to it, their nose warns them of any danger. Their long legs help them to run quickly away. A startled caribou can run at 50 miles per hour (80 km/h). They have to keep safe from people, wolves and bears, and also golden eagles, which kill newborn calves. They are also troubled by mosquitoes and warble flies and climb to higher and cooler places to escape them.

Caribou are herbivores and eat lichen, sedge and willow.

MORE ARCTIC ANIMALS

Parts of northern Asia, Europe and North America fall within the freezing Arctic region. Animals have thick coats and often change color to blend in with the snow. Animals like skunks, bears and chipmunks hibernate in a burrow during winter to conserve energy.

ARCTIC HARE

The Arctic hare has fur that helps it to hide. In winter, its long coat turns white. In summer, when the snow melts and the ground can be seen, it becomes a grayish-brown on top. Its large feet help it to run across the snow. Arctic hares live on rocky slopes in nests, since it is difficult to dig a burrow in the frozen Arctic ground. They eat different parts of the willow, grass, flowers and crowberries. Arctic hares gather in groups for protection. When a wolf or fox attacks, they scatter in different directions to confuse their attacker. This makes them look like big jumping snowballs. Each litter has four to eight dark-furred babies, born in June.

MUSK OX

The shaggy brown musk ox, which has hair even on its udders, wears one of the finest fur coats. Its 4-inch (10 cm) thick coat helps it survive the Arctic winter even at −30° F (−34° C). It feeds on any plant and grass it can find. Its horn covers the brain like armor. When the enemy attacks the ox spears it. Before a charge, it presses its nose against its knee to release the musk from a gland near the nose.

The Arctic hare's fur helps it to blend into its snowy surroundings.

Despite so much fur, the musk ox is sickened by diseases from mosquito bites on its nose.

22

🐾 *Wolverines have a gray-brown fur with a yellowish tinge around the face and on the sides.*

WOLVERINE

The wolverine isn't a cousin of the wolf. This shy but fierce animal is related to the weasel. It is clever and hides itself well. The wolverine, whose name means glutton, doesn't eat more than it needs, either. Although wolverines hunt, they also feed off dead animals and even if they find a large animal, they eat only as much as they need. They bury the rest in the snow to eat later. They spray what is left over with musk from special glands, to warn other animals not to touch it. Their large, furry feet help them to sprint at lightning speed over the snow to catch prey. They cannot see very well, but they can chase and tire out large prey like moose. At times they also climb on a rock and spring on the prey.

🐾 *The Arctic fox has fur on the soles of its feet to keep it warm.*

ARCTIC FOX

The Arctic fox lives further north than any other land mammal. It has the warmest fur of all Arctic animals. Its fur is gray-brown in summer, when the ice melts and the ground looks blotchy, and white in snowy winter. It has a long, bushy tail. It helps the fox steer when it runs. It can change direction quickly with a sweep of its tail. The tail also helps it to keep its nose and paws warm when it curls up to sleep. An Arctic fox hunts alone, and eats lemmings and birds.

CREATURE PROFILE

Common name:	Arctic fox
Scientific name:	*Alopex lagopus*
Height:	At shoulder 10-12 inches (25-30 cm)
Weight:	6-10 pounds (2.7-4.5 kg)
Color:	White in winter, Gray-brown in summer
Prey:	Lemming, tundra vole, birds

23

ANTARCTIC MARINE LIFE

The oceans in Antarctica have four times more plant and animal life per acre (ha) than the other oceans of the world. The cold water, rich in oxygen, encourages marine life. An obvious food chain works in the oceans—larger creatures eat smaller ones.

Fish

About 200 kinds of fish live in the Antarctic. The largest is Antarctic cod, which grows to 4.9 feet (1.5 m) and weighs 55 pounds (25 kg). Other fish include plunder fish, dragonfish, ice fish, eel-pouts, sea snails, rat-tailed fish, hagfish, barracuda, lantern fish and skates. Some Antarctic fish are the only vertebrates that have no hemoglobin in their blood. This makes their blood move more slowly, so they can save energy. Ice fish and cod can survive in the Antarctic because they have glycoproteins, or antifreeze, in their blood.

The luminous lantern fish lets out light like fireflies, through pores located on its head, underside and tail.

What's that light?

The first Antarctic fish was caught in 1840 during James Clark Ross's expedition. Several types of strange fish inhabit the oceans of Antarctica. Lantern fish have huge eyes and light-producing organs along their belly that attract prey. Patagonia toothfish have teeth like a dog's and a large mouth. Pouched lamprey stop feeding when they go into the freshwater to lay eggs, and die soon after their young are born. These fish eat krill, small plants and crabs.

Whales

Most of the whales found in the Antarctic in summer, head north in winter, since the water freezes over. There are two groups of whales in the Antarctic, six species of baleen whales and four species of toothed whales. Baleen is a hairy filter in the whale's mouth. It keeps the krill, small fish and other food in and allows the water the whale gulped in with the food to flow out. Baleens include the blue whale, the largest animal in the world. It grows up to 79 feet (24 m) and can weigh 140 tons (142.2 t). Other baleens are the fin, the southern right whale, the sei, the minke and the humpback. Toothed whales eat fish and squid and include the sperm whale, the smaller bottlenose whale, and the southern four-tooth whale.

KRILL

Krill are tiny shrimplike creatures. Antarctic krill is one of 85 species of krill found in the world. Krill swim in schools thousands of feet (m) wide and look like a red wave at the bottom of the sea. They rise to the surface only at night. They are important in the Antarctic food chain. Krill feed on diatoms, tiny algae that have a hard skeleton, algae and phytoplankton or tiny plants. Birds, fish, squid, seals and whales eat krill.

Krills can exist without food for 200 days!

CREATURE PROFILE

Common name:	Krill
Scientific name:	*Euphausia superba*
Length:	Adults: 2.7-3.1 inches (7-8 cm)
Weight:	0.03 ounces (1 g)
Enemy:	Man, fish, birds, seals, whales

Whales are mammals and breathe air through blowholes.

ARCTIC WHALES

Three types of whales spend their lives in the Arctic Ocean: bowhead, beluga and narwhal. Their bodies have enough blubber for them to survive the icy waters of the Arctic. All whales need to have a good sense of sound since the water is too cloudy to see well.

BOWHEAD

The bowhead whale gets its name from a large, bow-shaped head that is about 40 percent of its length. Its head is so strong that it can break through thick slabs of ice. It has a huge mouth, small eyes and large lips. Bowheads swim with their mouths open, eating along the way. A bowhead's mouth is lined with 350 pairs of black baleen plates and silver bristles. Bowheads feed mainly in summer when they swim north. They eat creatures like fish and shrimp, which are about 1 inch (2.5 cm) long. The food stays in their mouth while the water is filtered out through their baleen strainer.

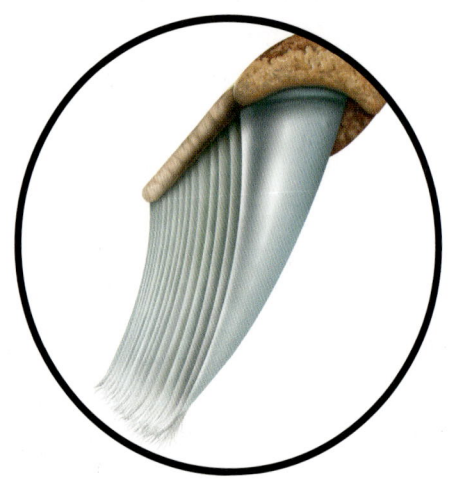

Baleens are thin, long plates of keratin, the edges of which have loose threads of keratine that act as fine filters. Each species has a unique color and size of baleen.

Singing whales

Bowheads swim in groups of three to 50. They normally dive for about 15 minutes and go as deep as 500 feet (155 m). Bowhead whales breathe through two blowholes at the top of their head. In autumn, they move south, where their babies are born. The calf, which is 17 feet (5 m) long and weighs about 5-6 tons (4.5-5.4 t) is born near the surface of the water. It can swim when it is less than half an hour old. The calf feeds on its mother's milk for a year. Bowheads sing or make different sounds, which cover seven octaves. This helps them find their way and keep together. They have a 20 inches (50 cm) layer of blubber that helps them survive the winter.

Sound and echoes help whales to communicate, hunt and find breathing holes.

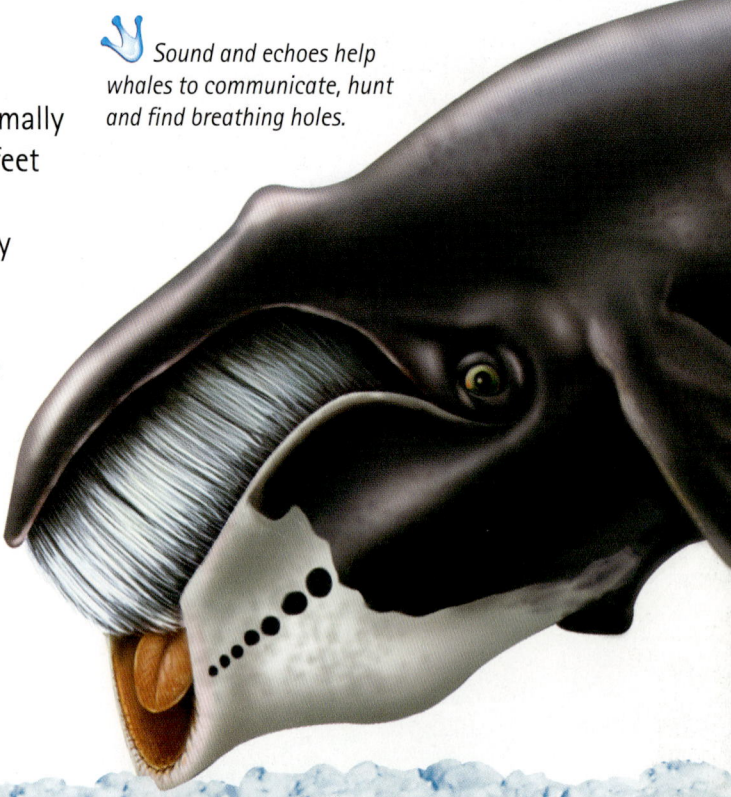

NARWHAL

Narwhal, in Old Norse, means "corpse whale," after its blue-gray skin with white blotches. The narwhal is an unusual whale. It has such a long ivory tusk that it has been mistaken for the magical unicorn of ancient legends. Narwhals have two upper teeth. When the male is one year old, its left tooth grows spirally, twisting counter-clockwise, for about 7–19 feet (2–3 m). They have a round head, a blunt snout, a small mouth and a cylindrical body covered with blubber. They live in pods of four to twenty, often in single-gender groups.

Noisy Narwhal!

Narwhals live for about 50 years. They are very vocal and noisy creatures that squeal, click and whistle to find each other and to navigate. Narwhals can dive and stay under the water for 7-20 minutes, while they look for squid, fish, shrimp and other small creatures. The calves have smooth brown skin and nurse for about four months.

CREATURE PROFILE

Common name:	Narwhal
Scientific name:	*Monodon monoceros*
Length:	Adult male: 16 feet (4.9 m)
	Adult female: 13 feet (4 m)
	At birth: 5 feet (1.5 m)
Weight:	Adult male: 1.8 tons (1,632 kg)
	Adult female: 1.1 tons (1,000 kg)
	At birth: 175 lb (80 kg)
Population:	About 45,000
Enemy:	Man, polar bear, orca, shark, walrus
Conservation status:	Endangered

The Narwhal probably uses its long tusk to fight in courtship battles. It also uses the tusk to look for food. However, the tusk is not used in hunting.

KILLER WHALE

Killer whales, or orcas, are the largest members of the dolphin family. They live in most oceans, but mainly in the Arctic and the Antarctic. They are smaller than many whales and have a body that tapers at both ends. Killer whales live in groups, or pods, of about 100. Female killer whales and calves swim at the center of the pod while males swim on the outside. They breathe through a blowhole on their head.

Killer whales have jet black bodies with white patches around their eyes, under the jaw, belly and on its sides.

Closing in for the kill

Killer whales eat fish, squid, seals, sea lions, walruses, birds, sea turtles, otters, penguins, polar bears, and even an occasional moose. They hunt in pods, pushing their prey into a small area before they attack. They can even kill a blue whale, the largest animal on earth. Sometimes, they slide onto sandbars or ice to chase their prey. They are toothed whales. Their 40 to 56 sharp teeth, each 3 inches (7.6 cm) long, lock together. These teeth are used for tearing. They can even swallow small seals and walruses whole.

Calf care

Killer whale calves are about 8.5 feet (2.6 m) long at birth and weigh between 300-400 pounds (136-181 kg). A baby can swim from the day it is born. For the first few days, the dorsal fin and tail flukes are flexible but as the calf ages, the fins grow stiff. A calf feeds from its mother for a year, although it cuts its first upper teeth at two or three months. The lower teeth appear when it is four months old and starts eating fish. When it is a few days old, the calf learns to make noises, and it improves its language as it grows.

I spy!

Killer whales have good eyesight, and can hear better than humans. Their fat-filled lower jawbone helps sound waves travel to their ears. Killer whales make clicking sounds and wait for the echo, so they can avoid hard objects in the dark and murky water. Their eyes are on each side of their head near a white false eyespot on their black body. The ears are small openings just behind the eyes. Their prey can mistake the eyespot for an actual eye and attack the spot instead of the whale's eyes. Killer whales lift their heads to see above the water. They do not have vocal cords, but killer whales can make a variety of sounds like clicks, moans, grunts, whistles and squeaks.

Fast swimmers

Killer whales swim faster than most mammals, reaching speeds of 30 miles per hour (48.4 km/h). They can dive 100-200 feet (30.5-61 m) and stay underwater for four to five minutes, when their heart slows down from 60 beats to 30 beats per minute. They inhale and close the flap over their blowhole before a dive. As they reach the surface, the blowhole opens and they breathe out. A layer of body fat, which is 3-4 inches (7.6-10 cm) thick, lies underneath the whale's skin and keeps it warm.

Killer whales are not threatened by any natural predators and therefore can live for about 50-80 years.

CREATURE PROFILE

Common name:	Killer whale
Scientific name:	*Orcinus orca*
Found in:	Largest numbers in Arctic and Antarctic regions
Weight:	Adult males: 8,000-12,000 pounds (3,628-5,442 kg)
	Adult females: 3,000-8,000 pounds (1,361-3,628 kg)
Length:	Adult males: 19-22 feet (5.8-6.7 m)
	Adult females: 16-19 feet (4.9-5.8 m)
Prey:	Fish, squid, seals, sea lions, walruses, birds, sea turtles, otters, penguins, polar bears
Status:	With about 70,000 to 180,000 in the Antarctic alone, killer whales are not an endangered species.

Despite being a predator and a killer, killer whales have never been reported to have killed a human being.

GREENLAND SHARK

The Greenland shark swims so slowly that it was named *somniosus microcephalus*, meaning "small-headed sleeper." Since it can live in very cold water 36-45° F (2-7° C), it is found in both the Arctic and Antarctic. Most Greenland sharks are 8-14 feet (2.4–4 m) long. The largest shark ever seen was 21 feet (6.5 m) long.

Black beauty

Little is known about this shark, since it prefers to live in deeper water than most sharks. This grayish-black shark with a short snout has a cylinder-shaped body and two small, boneless fins. Its teeth, framed by thin lips, are small for such a huge animal. However the teeth make up for their lack of size by being razor-sharp. The upper teeth are long, and the close-set lower teeth are flatter. The Inuit used the upper teeth as knives, and used the lower teeth to cut hair with.

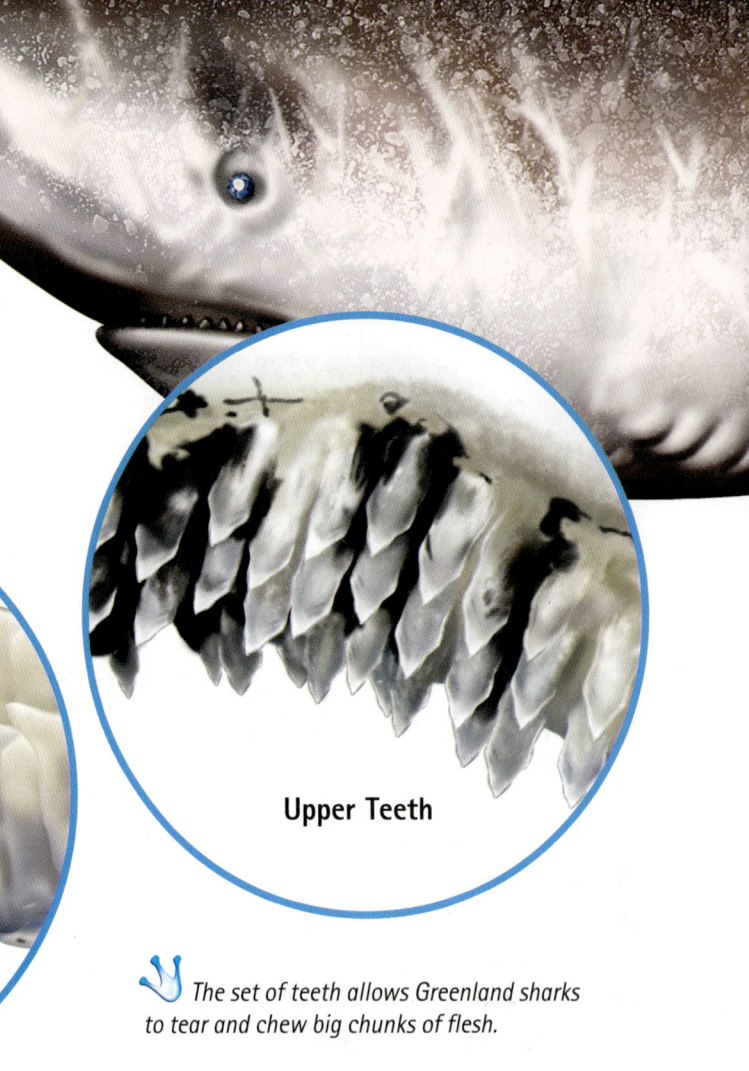

Upper Teeth

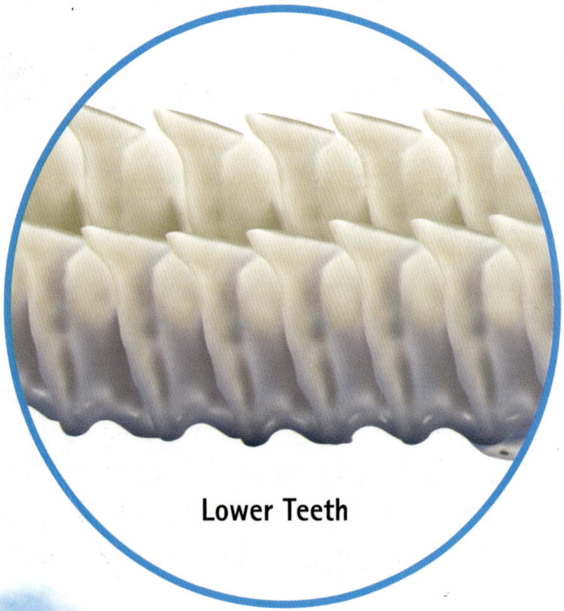

Lower Teeth

The set of teeth allows Greenland sharks to tear and chew big chunks of flesh.

Large family

Greenland sharks give birth to about ten pups at a time, which are about 15 inches (38 cm) long. Before birth, they develop from eggs inside the mother's body. They have short, wide tails that allow for quick bursts of speed, leading some biologists to believe that these sharks are not as sluggish as first thought. In winter, they go deeper into the sea. Female sharks are larger than males and the pups grow slowly, because of the very cold water they swim in.

CREATURE PROFILE

Common name:	Greenland shark
Other names:	Sleeper shark, gurry shark
Scientific name:	*Somniosus microcephalus*
Found in:	North Atlantic Ocean
Weight:	Adult 2,000 pounds (900 kg)
Length:	Adult 21 feet (6.5 m)
Prey:	Fish, seals, porpoises, flesh of dead animals
Enemies:	Man
Status:	Not endangered

The flesh of Greenland sharks can be poisonous to other animals.

Unusual oil well

Greenland shark liver is full of oil for which it is hunted. One shark can produce about 30 gallons (114 l) of oil. This oil helps the shark stay afloat and swim. The oil, rich in vitamins A and D, is said to be good for the health. The skin of the shark was used by the Inuit to make boots.

Strange friends

Glowing light-yellow copepods, tiny shrimplike creatures only 0.001 inch (3 mm) stick to this shark's small eyes. Although the sharks are often blinded by the copepods, the glow from them attracts prey. The Greenland shark eats fish such as herring, eels and salmon, seals, porpoises and even dead whales. They have only once been known to attack humans. Since they swim deeper than most other sharks at 1,300-2,000 feet (400-600 m) where very little light reaches, they use their sharp sense of smell to find food. When prey is near, they inhale, and the food, up to 3 feet (1 m) away, gets sucked into their mouth.

PENGUINS

Penguins are short-legged birds that can't fly. The name penguin was first given to the greak auk, a bird that looked like a penguin. It is now extinct. Does *penguin* derive from the word *pinion* (pinned wing)? Or the Welsh *pen gwyn* (white head)? Or the Latin *pinguis* (fat)? No one is sure.

Only Antarctica?

There are no penguins in the Arctic, perhaps because there are more hunters there. This includes bears, wolves, foxes, rats and people who hunted the great auk to extinction in the 1600s. Of the five species of penguins in Antarctica, the most common is the king penguin. It is the second largest in Antarctica. The Adelie penguin was named in 1840 by its discoverer, Dumont d'Urville, after his wife.

Just right for the cold

Penguin feathers are hard, small and packed closely together. The outer layer has long, smooth feathers that have a waterproof, oily coating. The inner layer of short, fluffy down traps the air and keeps them warm. Once a year, old feathers drop off, or molt. When they feel hot, penguins fluff out their feathers to let air pass through. An opening for an ear is hidden under the feathers on the head. On land, penguins can't see very far. They recognize each other by their voices. Penguins rest on their belly. Adelie and emperor penguins sleep standing up when they are warming an egg. Most newly hatched chicks are covered with soft down feather. These may be white, gray, black or brown. Since these are not waterproof the chicks must remain out of water.

Penguins use their small wings as flippers and paddle with webbed feet.

Look who's fishing!

Penguins catch prey with their beaks and swallow the food while they swim. They are good swimmers and can dive to 1,640 feet (500 m). They can stay underwater for several minutes and come up only to breathe. They have to stay safe from skuas, leopard seals and killer whales. A group of penguins is called a rookery. Male emperors that huddle together against winter storms are called a turtle, after the Roman soldiers' defensive position. Chicks group together in a crèche, which is a French word for crib.

What a din!

Penguins are noisy, smelly birds. Adelie penguins fight for nesting sites, for rocks and pebbles to make their nests or even if another penguin comes too close to their nests. They bray, sway, pinch with their beaks and hit the enemy with their bony flippers. They steal pebbles from other nests. When the chicks grow up and the penguins leave for the sea to feed, the last adult collects and hides pebbles for the next nest. This makes a bumper prize for the penguin that arrives first to nest! Penguins are clumsy walkers and cover ground by tobogganing on their stomachs. In the water, they play by jumping out and diving back in.

This is a rookery of penguins.

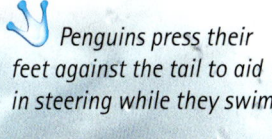
Penguins press their feet against the tail to aid in steering while they swim.

CREATURE PROFILE

Penguin

Scientific name:	*Spheniscidae*
Found in:	The southern hemisphere, right down to Antarctica
Weight:	Largest: adult emperor penguin, 60–90 pounds (27–41 kg)
	Smallest: adult fairy penguin, 2.2 pounds (1 kg)
Length:	Longest: adult emperor penguin 3.9 feet (1.2 m)
	Smallest: adult fairy penguin 16 inches (41 cm)
Prey:	Fish, krill, squid, crustaceans
Enemies:	Skua, leopard seal, killer whale, giant petrel, shark
Conservation status:	Stable

EMPEROR PENGUIN

The emperor penguin is the largest and heaviest penguin in the world. It has a big head with a black hood, short, black wings, a blue-gray neck patch, white front, orange ear patches and bill. Its tail is short. Emperors live throughout the year in Antarctica. They live up to 20 years.

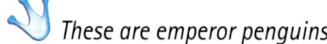 *These are emperor penguins.*

Proud papa

The emperors are the only birds in Antarctica that breed in winter. The female lays one egg in May on the snow when it can be as cold as -80° F (-62° C). She rolls it onto the male's feet. If he cannot scoop it up, it freezes. The male incubates the egg, covering it with his brood pouch, a fold of stomach skin. To keep the eggs warm, males huddle in groups called turtles.

Crèche

Both parents feed the chick, bringing up food from their stomachs. When the chicks are seven weeks old, they join a crèche or a group of chicks. Chicks are safe and warm in a crèche. When the parents come to feed them, the chicks recognize their call. Penguin calls can be heard a little over half a mile (1 km) away and help them find their families.

 *The mother leaves after laying eggs and returns after nine weeks to feed and raise the chick.*

34

Feast for a king

Unlike most penguins, which feed on krill or tiny shrimp, emperor penguins also eat fish and squid, which they catch in their sharp beaks. They can dive down to about 490-650 feet (150-200 m), and can stay under water for five to eight minutes. One dive was recorded at 700 feet (310 m), and another was 18 minutes long. That makes them the best divers among birds. Hungry chicks move their heads back and forth. When the parent looks down, the chick touches its beak and the parent feeds it.

Mom or Dad?

Male and female emperors look alike. Both lose weight while they nurse the chick, so it is difficult to tell them apart. The only difference is the female's squeakier voice. Emperors have a layer of blubber under their skin that keeps them warm. In the twentieth century, they were hunted for this fat. Chicks have extra down under their feathers. Emperors have more feathers than a flying bird. Their feathers are oily, smaller, stiff and are packed closely together.

CREATURE PROFILE

Common name:	Emperor penguin
Scientific name:	*Aptenodytes forsteri*
Found in:	Antarctica
Weight: adult:	Weight varies during breeding season in both male and female. Approx 60-90 pounds (27-41 kg)
Length:	Adult male 3.9 feet (120 cm)
	Adult female 3.75 feet (115 cm)
Prey:	Fish, squid, shelled creatures
Enemies:	Leopard seal, killer whale, giant petrel, shark
Population:	Estimated 200,000 breeding pairs, not counting birds younger than four years
Status:	Stable

The feathers help emperors wobble and slide on their bellies without getting wet.

At six months chicks go into the water and find their own food.

OTHER ANTARCTIC BIRDS

There are about 45 species of birds in the Antarctic region, of which 35 are birds that catch their food in the sea. They find krill, squid and fish in the water. They have few enemies on land, so their young are safe. As winter ends, Adelie penguins arrive, followed by petrels and skuas. Millions of birds celebrate summer here, including cormorants, pintails, gulls, terns, sheathbills, pipits and albatrosses. Most of them fly north in winter.

ALBATROSS

One of the largest birds on earth, wandering albatrosses are powerful flyers. They look for seafood near the surface of the water and can cover hundreds of miles (km), feeding at night. The mother lays a single egg, which is unusual for birds. Although they can live for about 50 to 60 years, thousands are killed by hunters. Wandering albatrosses get their name from their long flight, covering 6,213 miles (10,000 km) in 10 to 20 days. Some travel right around the earth. They arrive in Antarctica to breed in November, and settle in colonies on the grasslands, making nests of mud and grass. The eggs are laid in December. Parents incubate them until April, when it is winter in the Antarctic. The chicks are fed fish and squid. Albatrosses are white with black wavy lines on the breast, neck and upper back. Their bills are yellowish-pink. It takes a young bird nine years of wearing feathers of different colors to have the same color plumage as its parents.

CORMORANT

Cormorants are diving birds. They catch fish, eels, squid and even water snakes with a swift plunge into the water. They can dive up to 40 feet (12 m). Underwater, their feet propel them forward. Once back on land, they spread out their wings to dry since their dark feathers are not waterproof. They have a long, thin, sharp, hooked beak and four toes on their webbed feet. Cormorants nest in colonies on trees and cliffs. The eggs are light blue. Both parents look after the young.

Cormorants regurgitate food to feed their chicks.

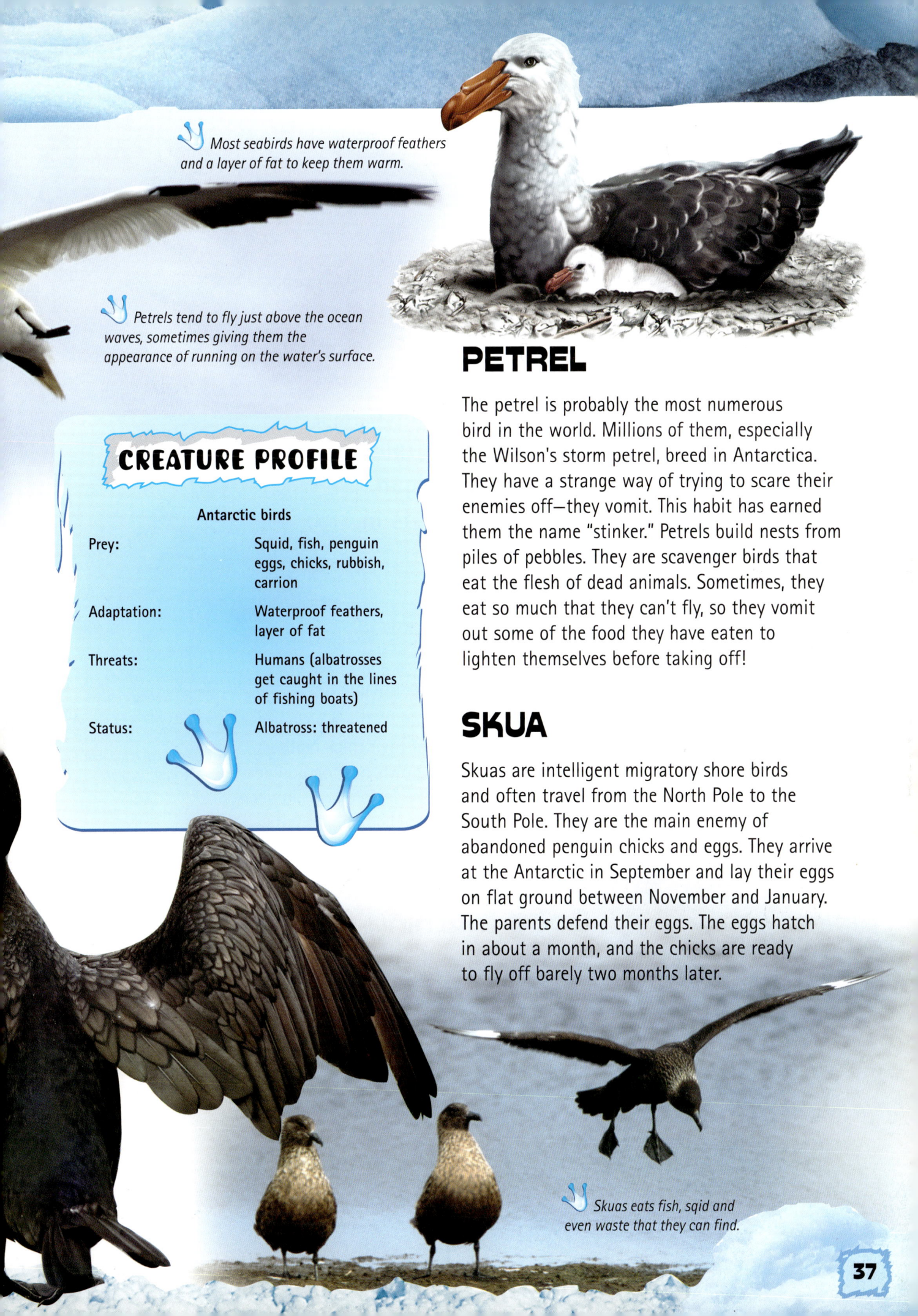

Most seabirds have waterproof feathers and a layer of fat to keep them warm.

Petrels tend to fly just above the ocean waves, sometimes giving them the appearance of running on the water's surface.

CREATURE PROFILE

Antarctic birds

Prey:	Squid, fish, penguin eggs, chicks, rubbish, carrion
Adaptation:	Waterproof feathers, layer of fat
Threats:	Humans (albatrosses get caught in the lines of fishing boats)
Status:	Albatross: threatened

PETREL

The petrel is probably the most numerous bird in the world. Millions of them, especially the Wilson's storm petrel, breed in Antarctica. They have a strange way of trying to scare their enemies off—they vomit. This habit has earned them the name "stinker." Petrels build nests from piles of pebbles. They are scavenger birds that eat the flesh of dead animals. Sometimes, they eat so much that they can't fly, so they vomit out some of the food they have eaten to lighten themselves before taking off!

SKUA

Skuas are intelligent migratory shore birds and often travel from the North Pole to the South Pole. They are the main enemy of abandoned penguin chicks and eggs. They arrive at the Antarctic in September and lay their eggs on flat ground between November and January. The parents defend their eggs. The eggs hatch in about a month, and the chicks are ready to fly off barely two months later.

Skuas eats fish, sqid and even waste that they can find.

SNOWY OWL AND FALCON

Millions of birds fly up to nest and bring up their young in the short Arctic summer. These include murres, snow geese, wagtails, sandpipers, ducks, gulls, loons, ptarmigan, gyrfalcon and snowy owls. As winter sets in, most fly to the warmer south.

SNOWY OWL

Harry Potter's pet, Hedwig, is a snowy owl. These are powerful birds. The males are all white while the females and the young have some dark feathers. These yellow-eyed owls can live in the cold because of their thick feathers, which even cover their feet. Snowy owls nest on boulders or even in unused eagle's nests. The female lays between five and fourteen eggs. These are laid on alternate days. The eggs hatch five weeks later.

During winters the snowy owl, gyrfalcon, ptarmigan and raven remain in the Arctic region.

Good morning or good evening?

In the Arctic, where there can be days of no darkness, the snowy owl hunts at all hours of the day for lemmings and other rodents and for the young of other birds. The snowy owl has a wide variety of calls, from an alarmed bark to something like a quack and even a musical note. They clap their powerful beak to scare away their enemies. The snowy owl's life cycle is dependent on the availability of lemmings, their main food.

Snowy owls can live in very cold temperatures.

GYRFALCON

The gyrfalcon is the largest falcon in the world. It is also one of the few birds whose feathers can range from a dark gray to white. The gyrfalcon is such a great hunter that in the Middle Ages, only a king was allowed to go hunting with one. It has claws and a hooked beak. They nest on ledges and even use empty nests of other birds. They lay three to five eggs that take a little over a month to hatch. The nestlings are ready to fly after about seven weeks.

Keen hunters

Gyrfalcons eat other birds, like the flightless ptarmigan and grouse, and small animals like squirrels and lemmings. They also prey on sea birds. Gyrfalcons have an unusual flight path. Just before they swoop down on their prey, they take a short flight up and then dive straight down. They are such accomplished hunters that they can grab prey even in midflight.

CREATURE PROFILE

Common name:	Gyrfalcon
Scientific name:	*Falco rusticolus*
Other names:	Adult male: jerkin
Found in:	Arctic region
Weight:	Up to 4.6 pounds (2.1 kg)
Length:	20–25 inches (50–63 cm)
Wingspan:	Up to 63 inches (160 cm)
Prey:	Smaller birds, squirrels, lemmings

The name gyrfalcon comes from the French *gerfaucon,* and is written in Medieval Latin as *gyrofalco.* Some say the name comes from the Old German word *giri,* which means "greedy."

FEATHERED VISITORS

Thousands of migratory birds visit the Arctic in summer to feed and nest. They take advantage of the long days when they can feed their young. Most migratory birds fly at night. Just before they migrate, they begin to get restless at dusk. This restlessness is known as *zugunruhe*. While they migrate, these birds face many dangers including bad weather. Many are also hunted down.

TUNDRA SWAN

The snow-white tundra swan is the largest bird in the Arctic. It has a long neck, short legs, a black bill with yellow spots, and black legs and feet. When they migrate, they fly all night. By May, they settle in the Arctic and nest on islands. They often return to an earlier nest. The swans pair for life and keep each other company throughout the year. The young are known as cygnets and it takes them a year to learn how to look after themselves. By early October, the swans are ready to leave the Arctic. They can fly at heights of 2,000–4,000 feet (609–1,200 m).

Other migratory birds that visit the Arctic include murres, snow geese and Arctic tern.

SIBERIAN CRANE

The Siberian crane is a large, white bird that has a red patch from its bill to behind its eye. Its legs are a light red. The female has a shorter beak. They spend most of their life in and around water. They even nest in marshy wetlands. Siberian cranes eat fruit and berries, rodents, fish and insects and also dig out roots and tubers from wetlands. As part of their mating ritual, a pair of cranes will dance and bow, flapping their wings while running and jumping to impress each other.

The Arctic tern has a thin, sharp, red beak and short red legs. It calls out in a high and sharp tone.

The savannah sparrow breeds in a wide variety of habitats including grasslands and cultivated land.

SAVANNAH SPARROW

The savannah sparrow is a little larger than your palm. This tiny bird flies up to 6,000 miles (9,656 km) a year. The sparrows fly at night, in groups of 10 to 100, and don't need to rest for hundreds of miles (km). They fly to the Arctic region to nest in late May or early June. The males try to impress the females by singing for them. Many savannah sparrows pair for life and like to nest close to their previous nest. They nest by tunnelling through the grass in order to try and keep their chicks safe. Sadly, predators discover many of their nests.

CREATURE PROFILE

Name:	Arctic tern
Scientific name:	*Sterna paradisaea*
Length:	12–15 inches (30–38 cm)
Weight:	1.98 pounds (900 g)
Color:	White, black head, orange beak, black under wings
Breeding:	1 to 3 eggs
Diet:	Fish, krill, insects

ARCTIC TERN

The Arctic tern is a sea bird that lives through an endless summer. It spends May and June in the Arctic and flies off to the Antarctic, spending November and December there, when it is summer there. They travel 12,000 miles (19,000 km) each way, meaning the Arctic tern travels further than any other bird and covers the equivalent distance of traveling to the moon and back in an average lifetime! The Arctic tern hunts by plunging into the sea to catch fish and often the male will offer part of his catch to the female.

ENDANGERING POLAR LIFE

Every year, about 6 billion tons (5.4 billion t) of carbon dioxide are released into the atmosphere. All animals breathe out carbon dioxide, a "greenhouse gas" that traps heat. Just as a greenhouse traps heat, carbon dioxide absorbs heat and doesn't let it go out into space. Many of our activities, like burning fossil fuel to run vehicles, also give off carbon dioxide. Some of it dissolves in water and some is converted into oxygen by plants and trees by photosynthesis.

Arctic

The temperatures at the poles have been rising every decade since the 1950s. In another fifty years, the poles could be 5-9° F (3-5° C) warmer. This rise is causing the ice caps in the Arctic to melt and the extra water is flooding rivers and seas. Intensive crop and cattle farming contribute to the problem both by encouraging deforestation and by increasing levels of methane, another greenhouse gas. Factories produce other gases that are heating the earth. As the earth is getting warmer, tree species of the south are moving north and are beginning to take over the tundra. If the quantity of greenhouse gases is not reduced, the tundra may disappear from the Arctic in another hundred years.

The increase in the level of carbon dioxide is leading to the warming up of the earth.

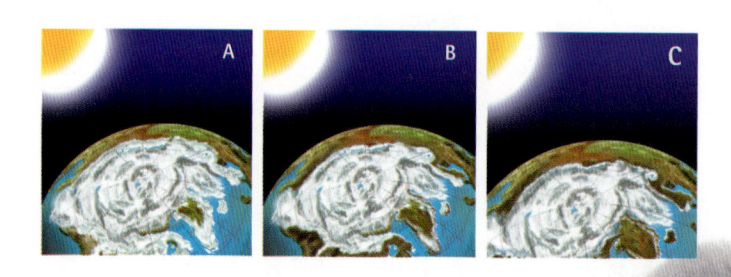

Departures in earth's temperature in degrees Celsius from the 1961-1990 average.

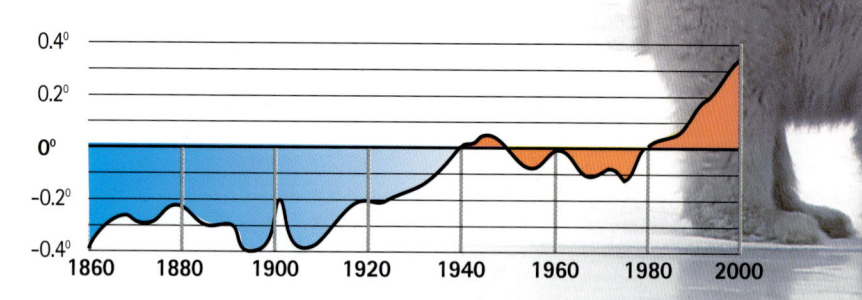

Sources: Intergovernmental Panel on Climate Change; Peter Webster et al. in September 16, 2005, issue of Science.

Antarctic

The temperature has risen 4.5° F (2.5° C) in northern Antarctica since 1945. Permanent ice shelves are melting. Ice shelves that previously melted annually have been melting increasingly earlier in the year for the past 20 years. If this continues, the west Antarctic ice sheet may melt. This would raise the sea level by as much as 19 feet (5.8 m). Many coastal areas, all over the world, would be flooded by this water, displacing millions of people and animals and destroying trees and habitats. In January 2002, the northern section of the Larsen-B ice shelf, an area of 1,250 square miles (3,250 sq km), collapsed. This was the largest collapse in 30 years. The permanent ice over the surface of Antarctica has been decreasing since the 1950s.

The melting ice is not only threatening life in the poles but will also have dangerous global effects.

Recent research has proved that polar bears have grown 10 percent thinner because the Arctic ice is melting faster each year and so the bears find it more difficult to hunt their prey.

Danger!

Polar bears walk along the ice to find food like seals, which play and live among the icebergs. Since ice in the Arctic is melting earlier than it used to, their paths are shrinking. Polar bears are 176-187 pounds (80-85 kg) lighter than they were 50 years ago because they find less food during the seven months they can feed themselves. Snow caves, where they nest, are collapsing before the cubs are able to put on enough blubber. As a result of the cold, cub deaths have risen 10 percent in the last 20 years. In the Antarctic, Adelie penguin populations have fallen 33-50 percent during the past 25 years since their winter homes are shrinking. While the population of seals, whales, polar bears and birds is falling, harmful insects are entering the polar regions because it is now less cold. These insects could spread disease, eat up the vegetation and destroy the ecosystem of the poles.

Glossary

Antifreeze (AN-tih-freez) Substances that are used to bring down the freezing point of mixtures

Blowholes (BLOH-hohlz) The nostrils through which whales breathe air. Baleen whales have two blowholes while toothed whales have a single blowhole

Breed (BREED) To reproduce

Breathing holes (BREETH-ing HOHLZ) Holes in the ice cover, created by sea mammals, through which they can surface to breathe

Clams (KLAMZ) A type of sea creature with shells and a soft interior

Cygnet (SIG-net) Young one of a crane

Ecosystem (EE-koh-sis-tem) All the living things in an area and how they affect each other and the environment

Extinction (ik-STINGK-shun) To exist no more

Greenhouse effect (GREEN-hows ih-FEKT) The absorption of solar heat by carbon dioxide, methane and water vapor present in the Earth's atmosphere

Glaciers (GLAY-shurz) A large mass of ice which moves slowly

Hemoglobin (HEE-muh-gloh-ben) A component of blood that contains iron and therefore lends red color to the blood

Hibernate (HY-ber-nayt) To sleep during winter to avoid the cold

Huddle (HUH-dul) To come close together in a group

Ice floes (YS FLOHZ) Frozen masses of sea water that float on the surface of the sea

Incubate (ING-kyuh-bayt) To keep eggs warm until the chicks come out

Inuit (IH-noo-wet) A group of people living in the Arctic regions of Siberia, Alaska and Greenland

Lemmings (LEH-mingz) Small ratlike creatures found in the Arctic regions

Glossary

Liverwort (LIH-ver-wort) Small plants like mosses which grow on wet surfaces

Mammals (MA-mulz) Warm blooded animals, the female of which gives birth to babies and feeds them her milk

Migrate (MY-grayt) To move from one region to another. Birds and animals migrate for suitable climatic conditions

Molt (MOHLT) To shed hair, feather, horns, shell or an outer layer of body periodically

Musk (MUSK) A fragrant substance secreted by the glands of some animals

Platypus (PLA-tih-pus) A semiaquatic mammal native to eastern Australia.

Predator (PREH-duh-ter) An animal that hunts, kills and eats other animals

Propel (pruh-PEL) To push or move something with force

Regurgitate (ree-GUR-juh-tayt) To bring out semidigested food back to the mouth

Ruminants (ROO-muh-nents) Hoofed animals that digest food in two steps. They first chew the food, then they regurgitate it with the help of four chambers in their stomach

Tobogganing (tuh-BAH-gun-ing) Falling rapidly

Vertebrates (VER-tuh-bruts) Creatures with backbones

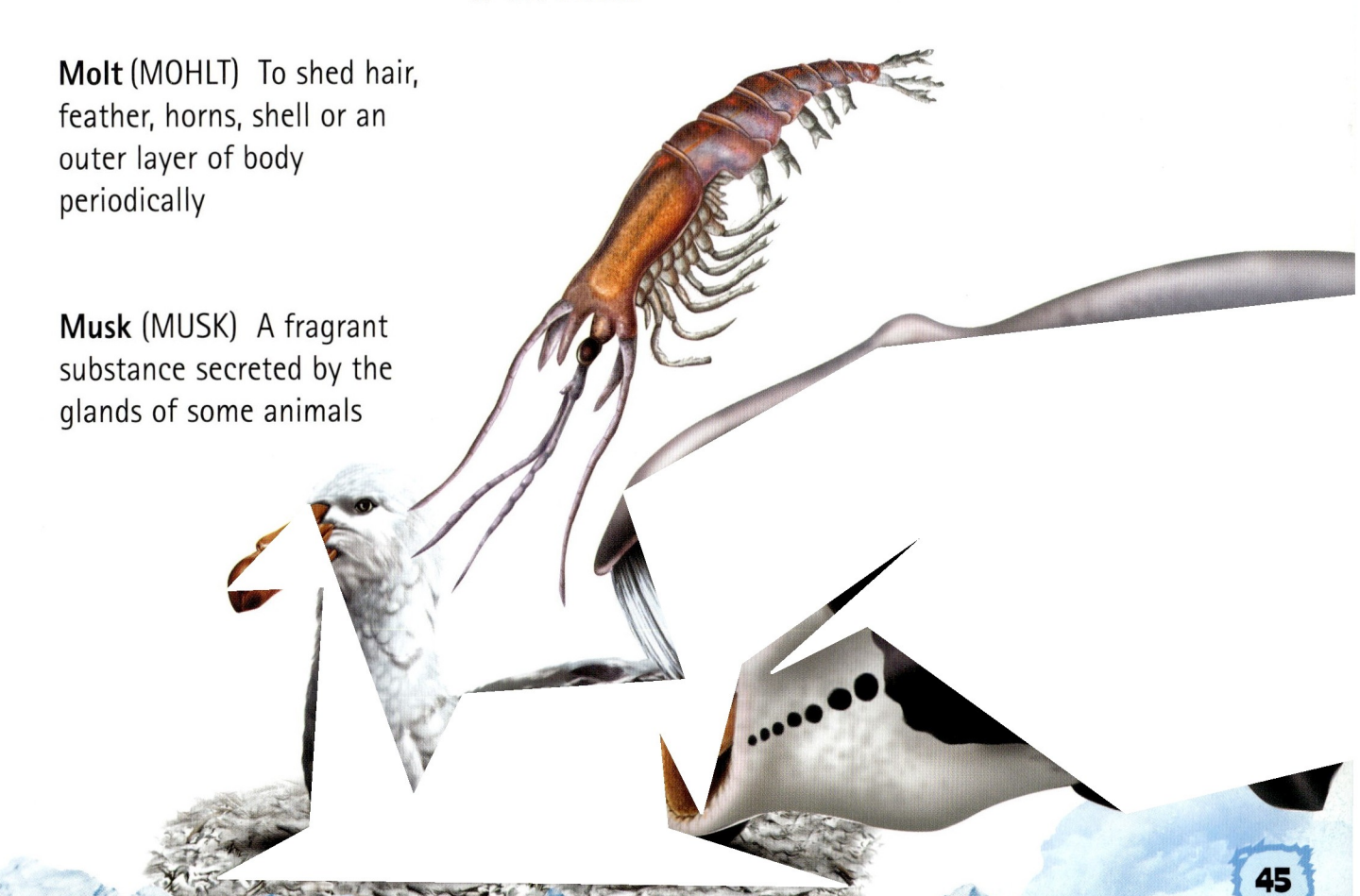

Further Reading & Web Sites

Mack, Lorrie. *Arctic and Antarctic*. New York: DK Publishing, Inc., 2006.

Rake, Jody Sullivan. *Walruses*. Rocheport, MO: Pebble Plus, 2007.

Squire, Ann O. *Polar Bears*. New York: Scholastic Library Publishing, 2007.

Swan, Erin Pembrey. *Penguins: From Emperors to Macaronis*. New York: Scholastic Library Publishing, 2003.

Tagliaferro, Linda. *Polar Bears*. Minnetonka, MN: T&N Children's Publishing, 2002.

Due to the changing nature of Internet links, PowerKids Press has developed an online list of Web sites related to the subject of this book. This site is updated regularly. Please use this link to access the list: www.powerkidslinks.com/wcre/polar/

Index

A
alabatross 36
ambush 23
Antarctic 6
antifreeze 24
antlers 20
Arctic 6
Arctic tern 41

B
blotchy 23
blowhole 28
blubber 12
bowhead whales 26
bray 33
breed 37
burrow 22

C
caribou 20
clams 18
cormorant 37
corpse 27
crabeater seal 15
crèche 34

D
den 11

E
ecosystem 43
emperor penguin 32
extinction 32

F
flippers 12

G
glaciers 7
glutton 23
greenhouse 42
Greenland shark 30
gyrfalcon 39

H
haemoglobin 24
huddle 34

I
ice floes 19
ice shelves 43
incubates 34

K
killer whale 28
krill 25

L
lantern fish 24
leopard seal 16
lemmings 23

M
mammal 18
migratory 37
molt 13
musk 22

N
narwhal 27

Index

P
penguin 32
photosynthesis 42
phytoplankton 25
pinion 32
pinnipeds 19
platypus 16
plumage 36
polar bear 8
predator 8
propel 36

R
regurgitate 36
ringed seals 10
rodents 38
ruminants 20

S
sanctuary 7
savannah sparrow 41
scavenger 37
seal 12
sluggish 31
snowy owl 38
squid 16
stalk 10
strainer 15

T
threat 17
tobogganing 33
tundra 6
tundra swan 40

V
vertebrates 24

W
walrus 18
webbed 9
Weddell seal 14
wolverine 23